AC

Paper F4 (ENG)

Corporate and business law

Pocket notes

ACCA
...AL PUBLISHER

KAPLAN
PUBLISHING

British library cataloguing-in-publication data

A catalogue record for this book is available from the British Library.

Published by:
Kaplan Publishing UK
Unit 2 The Business Centre
Molly Millars Lane
Wokingham
Berkshire
RG41 2QZ

ISBN 978-1-84710-790-9

Printed and bound in Great Britain.

Contents

Overview of the exam

There are ten questions on the paper and all of them are compulsory. Seven will be essay type questions. These are designed to **test your knowledge** of the law.

Three will be scenario based questions. These are designed to **test your ability** to apply the law to a factual scenario.

Each question may be divided into several parts.

Pilot paper

Essay questions	Scenario questions
Legal system	Contract law
Contract law	Share capital
Tort	Insider dealing
Registering a company	
Meetings	
Corporate governance	
Employment law	

Reading time – you will be allowed 15 minutes to read the paper and plan your answers.

Keys to success

Essay type questions

Questions of this type are simply looking for you to explain the relevant law. You should start with the general principle and then explain any exceptions. Support your answer with reference to case law, where possible.

Scenario questions

Questions of this type are looking for you to apply the law to a given scenario. You should initially tackle the question in the same way as an essay type question – state the general principle, explain any exceptions and support your answer with case law. Then, however, **you must refer to the facts of the scenario and explain how the law would be applied to those facts**.

Each question should take you no more than 18 minutes to complete.

Finally - When you think you have finished your answer, **re-read the question and read through your answer**. Have you covered everything that was required?

Legislation

Knowledge of new legislation is not expected until at least six months after the end of the month in which Royal Assent is given, or six months after the specific provision comes into effect, whichever is later.

chapter

1

Essential elements of the legal system

In this chapter

- Criminal law v civil law.
- The main English civil courts.
- Other courts.
- Sources of law.
- Judicial precedent.
- The hierarchy of the courts.
- Rules of statutory interpretation.
- Human Rights Act 1998.

Exam focus

There will always be one essay question on the English legal system in the exam paper.

Criminal law v civil law

Criminal law Civil law	Civil law
Criminal law relates to conduct which the State considers with disapproval and which it seeks to control. The object is to prove guilt.	Civil law is a form of private law and involves the relationships between individual citizens. The object is to show liability.
Purpose the enforcement of particular forms of behaviour by the State, which acts to ensure compliance.	Purpose to settle disputes between individuals and to provide remedies.
In criminal law the case is brought by the State in the name of the Crown. A criminal case will be reported as Regina v ..., where Regina means the latin for 'queen'.	In civil law the case is brought by the claimant, who is seeking a rememdy. The case will be referred to by the names of the parties involved in the dispute, such as Brown v Smith.
Burden of proof – guilt must be shown **beyond reasonable doubt**.	**Burden of proof** – liability must be shown on the **balance of probabilities**.
Object – to regulate society by the threat of punishment.	Object – usually financial compensation to put the claimant in the position he would have been in had the wrong not occurred.
The criminal court will sentence the defendant and it may fine him or impose a period of imprisonment.	The civil court will order the defendant to pay damages or it may order some other remedy, e.g. specific performance or injunction.

Exam focus

Underpinning question practice

To practice the basics use the following test your understanding:

- Complete/Essential Text – Chapter 1 Test your understanding 1.

The main English civil courts

House of Lords

5 Law Lords hear appeals from Court of Appeal and exceptionally from High Court

Court of Appeal

3 Lords Justices of Appeal hear appeals from the High Court and County Courts

County Court

First instance civil claims in contract, tort, landlord & tenant, probate and insolvency.
1 District judge hears small claims (max £5,000).
1 Circuit judge hears most fast-track cases (£5,000 - £15,000) and some multi-track cases (over £15,000 and/or complex cases).

High Court of Justice

1 High Court judge in first instance. 2-3 for appeals. Queens Bench Division hears first instance contract and tort multi-track claims. Chancery Division deals with land law, trusts, company law, partnership law, insolvency, etc. Hears appeals from County Courts on probate & insolvency. Family Division hears matrimonial cases.

Magistrates' court

Jurisdiction is mainly criminal (see section on criminal courts) but does have civil jurisdiction in family matters such as contact orders, adoption, and maintenance. There are also powers of recovery of council tax arrears and charges for water, gas and electricity.

Exam focus

Exam standard questions on this area can be found in the revision kit as follows:

- December 2002 – English Legal System.

Other courts

European Court of Justice	European Court of Human Rights
Deals with actions between the EU institutions and the member states. Ultimate authority on European Law. It is therefore superior to the House of Lords. Cases are referred to it by national courts.	The final court of appeal in relation to matters concerning the Human Rights Act 1998. Must have exhausted proceedings in the English courts before ECtHR will hear case
No appeal.	No appeal.

The main criminal courts

House of Lords

Five Law Lords hear appeals from the Court of Appeal and exceptionally from High Court.

Court of Appeal

Three Lord Justice of Appeal hear appeals from the Crown Court

Crown Court

Presided over by a judge whose role is to decide questions of law and impose the punishment.

Case will be heard before a jury whose role is to decide questions of fact i.e. whether defendant is guilty of the offence.

Magistrates Court

Court of first instance. Deals with criminal cases in various ways:

- Summary offences – decides whether defendant is guilty of the offence and imposes the penalty.
- Indictable offences where there is to be trial by jury. Magistrates will conduct committal proceedings to make sure the defendant has a case to answer.

Presided over by either:

- Lay Magistrates. The bench usually consists of three.
- Stipendiary Magistrate sitting alone.
- Appeals on questions of fact fo to the Crown Court.
- Appeals on questions of law go to the high Court.

High Court (Queens Bench Division)

Three judges preside.

Hears appeals from Magistrates Court on points of law.

Appeals go directly to the House of Lords.

Exam focus

Exam standard questions on this area can be found in the revision kit as follows:

- June 2007 – Types of law.

Sources of law

Case law	Legislation
Common law • Introduced the system of precedent. • The only remedy was damages. • Rigid and inflexible.	**Direct legislation** = Acts of Parliament. A Bill must go through the following stages in both the House of Lords and the House of Commons: 1st reading, 2nd reading, committee stage, report stage, 3rd reading, Royal Assent.
Equity • Began as a form of appeal. • More flexible than the common law. • Introduced new discretionary remedies such as injunctions and specific performance. • Concerned with fairness. Equitable remedies are not available as of right. Must meet the **maxims of equity**: e.g. • He who seeks equity must have acted equitably; and • delay defeats equity.	**Indirect legislation** = delegated legislation. Consists of: • **Statutory instruments** - Made by Government Ministers using powers delegated by Parliament • **Bye-laws** - Made by local authorities • **Orders in Council** - Made by the Privy Council in the name of the Monarch on the advice of the Prime Minister.

Exam focus

Exam standard questions on this area can be found in the revision kit as follows:

- June 2006 – Delegated legislation.
- June 2008 – Sources of law.

Judicial precedent

Ratio decidendi	Obiter dicta
The legal reason for the decision	Statements which are not part of the ratio
The ratio is capable of forming the binding precedent	Persuasive rather than binding precedent

The hierarchy of the courts

House of Lords – Binds all lower courts. From 1966 does not bind itself.

Court of Appeal - Binds all lower courts and itself unless earlier decision overruled or inconsistent with European law. Not bound by own criminal decisions.

High Court – Not bound by its own decisions, but strong persuasive authority.

Advantages of judicial precedent – consistency, flexibility, practical.

Disadvantages – complex, restricts judges' discretion. However, judges retain discretion by 'distinguishing on the facts' or overruling lower courts.

Exam focus

Exam standard questions on this area can be found in the revision kit as follows:

- June 2004 – Binding Precedent.
- June 2005 – Doctrine of Precedent.

Underpinning question practice

To practice the basics use the following test your understanding:

- Complete/Essential Text – Chapter 1 Test your understanding 2.

Rules of statutory interpretation

Literal rule	Golden rule	Mischief rule	Purposive Rule
Words must be given their ordinary grammatical meaning, even if it produces an undesirable outcome.	Used where the literal rule gives more than one meaning or provides an absurd result. Involves choosing the meaning that produces the least absurd result.	Used to interpret a statute in a way which provides a remedy for the mischief the statute was enacted to prevent.	The purpose of an Act was to provide for the safe storage of film wherever it might be stored on 'premises'. The claimant argued that 'premises' did not include a cave and so the Act had no application to this case.
Fisher v Bell – It was a criminal offence to 'offer for sale' a flick-knife. A shopkeeper who displayed one in his shop window was held not guilty as the court chose to follow the contract law meaning of the word 'offer'.	**Adler v George** – The words 'in the vicinity of' a prohibited place' in the Official Secrets Act were held to cover the acts of the defendant which took place 'within' a prohibited place.	**Gorris v Scott** – As the purpose of the statute was to prevent the spread of contagious disease and not guard against the danger of the property being washed overboard, the claim failed.	**Gardiner v Sevenoaks RDC (1950)** – The purpose of the Act was to protect the safety of persons working in all places where film was stored. If film was stored in a cave, the word 'premises' included the cave.

Note also – **Euisdem generis** – general words mean the same kind of thing as the specific words they follow. **Expressio unio est exclusio alterius** – a statute which expresses particular things by implication excludes everything else.

Human Rights Act 1998

What is its purpose?	The HRA 1998 incorporates the European Convention for the Protection of Human Rights and Fundamental Freedoms into UK domestic law.
What is convention law?	Convention law = the Convention + decisions of the European Court of Human Rights.
How does it affect judicial interpretation?	UK courts must take Convention law into account when deciding a question which has arisen in connection with a Convention right.
Any impact on the doctrine of precedent?	Judges will not be bound by a previous interpretation of existing legislation where it did not take into account Convention rights - **Mendoza v Ghaidan (2003)**.
What if legislation is incompatible with the Convention?	The courts cannot declare primary legislation invalid. They can only make a declaration of incompatibility and leave it to Parliament to remedy the situation through new legislation. However, the courts do have the power to declare secondary legislation (e.g. statutory instruments) invalid.
What is derogation?	A derogation is a provision which allows for all or part of a legal measure to be applied differently, or not at all.

chapter

2

Contract law

In this chapter

- Offer.
- Acceptance.
- Intention to enter legal relations.
- Consideration.
- The part-payment problem.
- Terms.
- Exclusion clauses.
- Breach of contract.
- Remedies for breach of contract.

Exam focus

Contract law is a very important area of the syllabus. There are likely to be two questions, one of which will be of a scenario type.

Offer

Definition

An offer is a definite and unequivocal statement of willingness to be bound on specified terms without further negotiations. Once accepted it forms a valid contract.

It can be made to a particular person, to a class of persons or even to the whole world: **Carlill v Carbolic Smoke Ball Co**.

What is not an offer?

- A mere statement of selling price in response to a request for info.
- An invitation to treat = an invitation to the other party to make an offer; e.g. **Gibson v Manchester City Council**: 'we may be prepared to sell'.

Examples of invitations to treat

- Most adverts – **Partridge v Crittenden** (advert for rare birds).
- Shop window displays – **Fisher v Bell** (flick-knives).
- Goods on shop shelves – **Pharmaceutical Society of GB v Boots**
- Tenders.

How does an offer terminate?

- **Revocation** by the offeror at any time before acceptance, even if agreed to keep open. However, must be communicated to offeree by offeror or reliable third party.
- **Rejection** by the offeree – either outright or by a counter-offer – **Hyde v Wrench**.
- **Lapse** – on death of offeror or offeree, or after expiry of fixed time.

Exam focus

Exam standard questions on this area can be found in the revision kit as follows:

- December 2004 – Offers and Tenders.
- June 2008 – Invitation to Treat.

Underpinning question practice

To practice the basics use the following test your understanding:

- Complete/Essential Text – Chapter 2 Test your understanding 2.

Acceptance

Definition

Acceptance is the unqualified and unconditional assent to all the terms of an offer. It can be oral, written or by conduct: **Carlill v Carbolic Smoke Ball Co**.

Communication

- Acceptance is not effective until communicated to offeror – **Entores v Miles Far Eastern**.
- Offeror can stipulate particular mode of acceptance. However, if merely requests a mode, offeree not limited to that mode.
- Offeror can't stipulate that silence is acceptance – **Felthouse v Bindley**.
- Offeror can expressly or impliedly dispense with need for communication.

The postal rule

- An exception to the general rule that acceptance must be communicated.
- Acceptance is complete as soon as letter posted – **Adams v Lindsell**.
- Postal rule applies even if letter never received – **Household Fire Insurance v Grant**.
- Only applies if letter properly stamped and addressed and if post is reasonable method of communication.
- Does not apply if offeror states he must actually receive the acceptance.

Exam focus

Exam standard questions on this area can be found in the revision kit as follows:

- June 1998 – Terms used in the law of contract.
- December 2007 – Ali.

Underpinning question practice

To practice the basics use the following test your understanding:

- Complete/Essential Text – Chapter 2 Test your understanding 3.

Consideration

Definition

'Consideration is an act or forbearance (or the promise of it) on the part of one party to a contract as the price of the promise made to him by the other party to the contract' – **Dunlop v Selfridge**.

'Some right, interest, profit or benefit accruing to one party, or some forbearance, detriment, loss or responsibility given, suffered or undertaken by the other'- **Currie v Misa**.

Types of consideration

- Executory consideration is given where there is an exchange of promises to do something in the future.
- Executed consideration means that the consideration is in the form of an act carried out at the time the contract is made.
- Past consideration – this is an act which has been wholly performed before the other party gives his promise.

General rule	**Consideration must not be past**
Re McArdle	Husband & wife repaired house. Held work could not support a later promise to reimburse the cost.
Re Casey's Patents	Exception – a request for services may be treated as an implied promise to pay, even if actual promise not made until later.

General rule	**Consideration must be sufficient but need not be adequate**
Chappell & Co. v Nestlé	Records sold for 1s 6d plus 3 chocolate wrappers. Wrappers were part of the consideration even though they had minimal value.
Thomas v Thomas	Promise to convey house to widow for rent of £1 a year was binding. The consideration had value, even though inadequate.
White v Bluett	Son's promise to stop complaining did not amount to consideration as not valuable.
General rule	**Performance of an existing statutory duty is not consideration**
Collins v Godefroy	A witness was promised payment if he would attend court and give evidence. No consideration as legally required to attend court.
Glasbrook Bros. v Glamorgan CC	Exception – action exceeding statutory duty is consideration. Company required the police to provide protection in excess of statutory requirement. Held: police had provided sufficient consideration to give entitlement to remuneration.
General rule	**Performance of existing contractual duty is not consideration**
Stilk v Myrick	Captain promised to share wages of deserting seamen with rest of crew. Not binding as no extra consideration from seamen.
Williams v Roffey Bros.	Exception – R offered W extra money to complete work on time. Although W did no extra work, held sufficient consideration as enabled R to avoid penalty clause. Also, no pressure by W to make R offer the extra money.

Exam focus

Exam standard questions on this area can be found in the revision kit as follows:

- December 2002 – Consideration.

Underpinning question practice

To practice the basics use the following test your understanding:

- Complete/Essential Text – Chapter 2

  Test your understanding 4.

The part-payment problem

The rule in Pinnel's case – states that payment of a lesser sum, in satisfaction of a greater sum, cannot be satisfaction for the whole sum.

Exceptions

- Variation of terms at the creditor's request (with accord and satisfaction).

E.g. payment on an earlier date.

- Part-payment by a third party.
- Equitable doctrine of promissory estoppel prevents a person going back on his promise to accept a lesser amount – **Central London Property Trust v High Tree House**.

Limitations on promissory estoppel:

- It is a 'shield not a sword', i.e. it can only be used as a defence.
- It may only have suspensory effect, i.e. if give notice, can insist on future payments in full.
- 'He who comes to equity must come with clean hands', i.e. party seeking to rely on promissory estoppel must have acted fairly.

Exam focus

Exam standard questions on this area can be found in the revision kit as follows:

- December 2002 – Ball Ltd.

Intention to create legal relations

A contract does not exist unless the parties intend it to be legally enforceable. The law presumes the intention of the parties based on the type of agreement. The presumption can be rebutted by clear evidence to the contrary.

Domestic or social agreements	Commercial agreements
Presume no intention to be legally bound	Presume intention to be legally bound
Balfour v Balfour – Husband promised wife monthly allowance. Not legally binding as domestic arrangement.	**Jones v Vernon's Pools** – Wording of contract stated 'binding in honour only'. Therefore no intention to be legally bound.
Simpkins v Pays – Competition entry between Pays, granddaughter and lodger. Presumption rebutted as clearly intended to share prize money.	
Merritt v Merritt – Presumption rebutted as husband and wife separated.	

Exam focus

Exam standard questions on this area can be found in the revision kit as follows:

- December 2004 – Alan and Cath.
- December 2007 – Doctrine of Privity.

Terms

Terms v representations – A representation is something that is said by the offeror in order to induce the offeree to enter into the contract. It may or may not become a term of that contract.

Types of terms

Conditions	Warranties	Innominate terms
An important term going to the root of the contract.	Less important term, incidental to main purpose.	Indeterminate – neither a condition nor a warranty.
Breach can result in damages or discharge.	Breach results in damages only.	Remedy depends on effects of breach.
Poussard v Spiers – opera singer failed to appear on opening night. Held: breach of condition entitling injured party to treat contract as ended.	**Bettini v Gye** – opera singer failed to attend rehearsals. Held: breach of warranty. Injured party could not treat contract as ended. Damages only.	**The Hansa Nord** – some of ship's cargo arrived in poor condition. Buyer rejected whole cargo. Held: only remedy was damages. Breach insufficient to justify treating contract as ended.

Sources of terms

Express – contained in contract; written or oral.
Implied – by statute, by the courts if necessary to give business efficacy, by the nature of the contract, by custom and usage.

Exam focus

Exam standard questions on this area can be found in the revision kit as follows:

- December 2002 – Express and implied terms
- December 2003 – Conditions, warranties and innominate terms.

Underpinning question practice

To practice the basics use the following test your understanding:

- Complete/Essential Text – Chapter 2 Test your understanding 5.

Exclusion clauses

Definition

A term that seeks to exclude a party's liability for breach of contract.

Common law rules	
Must be incorporated into contract – by signature, notice or previous dealings.	
L'Estrange v Graucob	Clause incorporated by **signature**, even if the signatory did not read or understand the document.
Curtis v Chemical Cleaning	**Exception** – signature does not incorporate clause if effect of term was misrepresented. Liability for damage to wedding dress not excluded due to misrepresentation of clause.
Olley v Marlborough Court	Clause incorporated by **notice**, provided given **before making the contract**. Notice in hotel room did not exclude liability as contract made at reception desk.
Spurling v Bradshaw	Clause incorporated by **consistent course of dealings** between parties on terms which included exclusion clause.
Hollier v Rambler Motors	Three or four deals between a garage and private customer over a five-year period insufficient to constitute course of dealing.

Wording must cover loss – contra proferentum rule interprets clause narrowly	
Photo Productions Ltd. v Securicor	Contract to provide security for factory excluded liability for 'any injurious act or default by any employee'. Security guard burned factory down. Clause valid as wording unambiguous.

Does the clause pass the common law rules? If no, the clause is void. If yes, consider statutory rules.

If the contract is made in the course of business, UCTA 1977 applies.

Void if exempts liability for death or personal injury.
Other loss – void unless 'reasonable'.

If one party is a consumer and the other is in business, UTCCR 1999 applies in addition to UCTA 1977.

Unfair (and not binding) if not expressed in plain language or if it causes an imbalance in parties' rights to the detriment of the consumer.

Burden of proving reasonableness is on party seeking to rely on clause.

In assessing whether a term is unfair/unreasonable, the Court has regard to:

- the strength of the bargaining positions of the parties
- whether the buyer received an inducement to agree to the term
- whether the goods were supplied to the special order of the customer
- whether the buyer knew or ought to have known of the existence of the term
- the extent to which the seller dealt fairly and equitably with the consumer.

Exam focus

Exam standard questions on this area can be found in the revision kit as follows:

- June 2002 – Exclusion clauses
- June 2004 – Amy.

Underpinning question practice

To practice the basics use the following test your understanding:

- Complete/Essential Text – Chapter 2

  Test your understanding 6.

Breach of contract

Definition – Breach of contract occurs where one of the parties fails to carry out the terms of the contract in the manner required by the contract.

Actual breach	• becomes apparent at or after the time set for performance.
Anticipatory breach	• occurs before performance. • may be **express**, e.g. one party declares they have no intention of performing the contract. • may be **implied**, e.g. one party does something which makes performance impossible. • the innocent party can choose to wait until the due date for performance before taking action. However, he runs the risk of the contract being discharged for some other reason.

Consequences of breach

Damages	• available for breach of any contract.
Treat contract as discharged	• available for breach of condition or where other party has made an anticipatory breach.

Remedies for breach of contract

Damages

- Common law remedy. Available as of right for breach of contract.
- Aim to put injured party in position would have been in if contract properly performed.
- Intended to be compensatory not punitive.
- **Liquidated damages** – genuine pre-estimate of expected loss. Enforceable by court.
- **Penalty clause** – Threatens large damages for breach. Unenforceable.

Remoteness of loss

Hadley v Baxendale	General damages arise naturally from the breach. Special damages do not occur in the normal course of things, but were reasonably in the contemplation of the parties, at the time they made the contract, as the probable result of the breach.
Victoria Laundries v Newman	Delay in delivery of boiler caused loss of normal trading profit, plus an extra large profit on the loss of a government contract. Held: could recover damages for first loss, but not second as unknown to defendant i.e. too remote.
Jarvis v Swan Tours	Can't usually recover for loss of enjoyment, unless contract is one designed to give enjoyment.

Measure of damages

•	Damages for **loss of bargain** put claimant in position would have been in if the contract had been performed. If no actual loss, recover only nominal damages.
•	**Reliance damages** enable claimant to recover compensation for expenses incurred in performing his part of contract before breach – **Anglia TV v Reed**.
•	Claimant must **mitigate loss** – **Brace v Calder**.
•	Difficulty in evaluating losses does not prevent their recovery.

Other remedies

Specific performance	Requires someone to perform their contractual obligations. Not available for personal service contracts. Equitable remedy.
Injunction	Orders someone to do something or not to do something. Equitable remedy.

Equitable remedies are discretionary – not granted if damages are an adequate remedy or if claimant acted unfairly.

Exam focus

Exam standard questions on this area can be found in the revision kit as follows:

- December 2003 – Damages and mitigating losses
- June 2004 – Damages
- December 2005 – Anticipatory breach
- June 2008 – Bild Ltd.

Underpinning question practice

To practice the basics use the following test your understandings:

- Complete/Essential Text – Chapter 2

  Test your understanding 6
  Test your understanding 7
  Test your understanding 8
  Test your understanding 9.

chapter

3

Tort

In this chapter

- The tort of negligence.
- Negligence by professionals.
- The tort of 'passing off'.

Exam focus

There is always one question on the law of torts in the exam.

The tort of negligence

Definition

A tort is a type of civil wrong: e.g. negligence, trespass. It is a breach of a legal duty or infringement of a legal right which gives rise to a claim for damages. For an action for negligence to succeed, the claimant must show three things, that:

- A duty of care was owed to them by the defendant.
- There was a breach of that duty.
- The resulting damage was principally caused by the negligence.

Duty of care

- The existence of a duty of care is a question of law.
- One owes a duty of care to one's neighbour **(Donoghue v Stevenson)**

Definition of neighbour

'...persons who are so directly affected by my act that I ought reasonably to have them in contemplation'.

The limits of the duty of care

In the case of The Nicholas H (Marc Rich & Co v Bishops Rock Marine) (1995), four tests were laid down which should be followed in determining whether a duty of care exists.

The issues to be considered are:

- Was the damage reasonably foreseeable by the defendant at the time of the act or omission?
- Is there a neighbourhood principle or sufficient proximity (closeness) between the parties?
- Should the law impose a duty of care between the parties i.e. is it fair and reasonable to do so?
- Is there a matter of public policy which exists or requires that no duty of care should exist?

The Nicholas H case focused on financial loss, but these tests should also be applied when determining the duty of care for physical damage cases.

Breach of that duty

- Normally the claimant must show that the defendant has been negligent. The test is that of the 'reasonable man' (**Blyth v Birmingham Waterworks Co**).
- Lack of skill is no defence.
- There is no negligence if reasonable precautions have been taken.
- The courts do take the surrounding circumstances into account.

Exam focus

Exam standard questions on this area can be found in the revision kit as follows:

- June 2008 – Standard of care.

Underpinning question practice

To practice the basics use the following test your understandings:

- Complete/Essential Text – Chapter 3

  Test your understanding 1

  Test your understanding 2

  Test your understanding 3

  Test your understanding 4

  Test your understanding 5.

Resulting damage

- The damage must be a direct consequence of the negligence. If the accident would have occurred anyway, the causal link is not established.
- The damage must have been reasonably foreseeable at the time of the negligence. It must not be too remote.

Exam focus

Exam standard questions on this area can be found in the revision kit as follows:

- December 2007 – Remoteness of damage.

Negligence by professionals

Hedley Byrne v Heller established that a professional person owes a duty of care to any person he knew or reasonably ought to have known would rely on his professional statement. Liability is only owed when:

- the proximity test is satisfied. The defendant must have known that the information would be communicated to the plaintiff, used for a particular purpose and relied upon by the plaintiff
- the floodgate test applies. The courts will only make the defendant liable when it is reasonable to do so in the public interest.

Caparo Industries v Dickman applied the proximity and floodgate tests to auditors and held that the auditor is not liable to third parties.

When the auditor gives his audit report to the shareholders he is fulfilling a statutory role and it would be unreasonable to make him liable to anyone other than the shareholders as a body. So if he is negligent only the company can sue him. Individual shareholders and third parties cannot.

However if the auditor gives specific assurances to a third party, he is liable to that third party if the assurance is given negligently.

An accountant is expected to follow the requirements of accounting standards and the code of conduct of his professional body.

In **JEB Fasteners v Marks, Bloom & Co.** accountants were held to be negligent for not following normal accountancy practice.

Defences

Contributory negligence	The court may reduce any damages it awards to the claimant, depending on the degree to which he is judged responsible for his own loss.
Volenti non fit injuria	If a person has freely consented to a negligent act he cannot obtain a remedy.
Act of God	Something which occurs in the course of nature, which was beyond human foresight and against which the defendant could not have been expected to provide.
Exclusion clauses	If valid is a viable defence. But need to consider if it falls within the provision of the Unfair Contract Terms Act 1977.

Exam focus

Underpinning question practice

To practice the basics use the following test your understandings:

- Complete/Essential Text – Chapter 3

  Test your understanding 6

  Test your understanding 7.

The tort of 'passing off'

The tort arises:

- where one business uses a name which is similar to that of an existing business; and
- it misleads persons into believing that they are the same business; and
- it causes actual damage to that business or will probably do so.

Remedy

If proved, the court may restrain the business from trading under that name and order that damages be paid to the person whose business has suffered loss.

Ewing v Buttercup Margarine Company

Ewing owned the well-known Buttercup Dairy Company. He succeeded in restraining the Buttercup Margarine Company from using that name. The court held that the word 'Buttercup' was so closely associated with Ewing dairy products as to be likely to cause confusion if used by the similar, but unconnected, margarine business.

If a company feels than another company has a name which is too similar to its own, it may object to the Company Name Adjudicator under CA 06. The Adjudicator will consider the case and then make their decision. In most cases the Adjudicator will require a name change, and in some cases the Adjudicator may state the new company name.

chapter

4

Employment law

In this chapter

- Employed v self-employed.
- Common law duties.
- Wrongful dismissal.
- Unfair dismissal.
- Constructive dismissal.
- Redundancy.
- Remedies.

Exam focus

There is likely to be one question on employment law. It could be either an essay question or a scenario question.

Employed v self-employed

Employee	Independent contractor
Works under a contract of service	Works under a contract for services
• **control test** (old) - employee is subject to control by employer as to how, where and when he does his work: **Yewens v Noakes** • integration test = employee if work is integrated into business, not merely accessory	• economic reality test - (multiple test): Worker is in business on own account if he provides own tools, is able to delegate, works for a number of clients, suffers a degree of financial risk as hours and payment are irregular, etc. **Ready Mixed Concrete v Ministry of Pensions**

Importance of difference
• employees receive statutory protection (e.g. unfair dismissal/redundancy) • implied terms in contract of employment (e.g. duty of obedience) • vicarious liability only applies to acts of employees • insolvency – employee is preferential creditor; self-employed is ordinary unsecured creditor • pay of employees is net of income tax and national insurance under PAYE system • state benefits (e.g. statutory sick pay) only available to employees

Exam focus

Exam standard questions on this area can be found in the revision kit as follows:

- June 2006 – Gus and Hilda
- June 2008 – Employment contracts.

Underpinning question practice

To practice the basics use the following test your understanding:

- Complete/Essential Text – Chapter 4
  Test your understanding 1.

Common law duties

Duties of employee	Duties of employer
• **Obey lawful and reasonable orders.** **Pepper v Webb**. A gardener refused to plant the plants when instructed by the employer. **Held**: He was in breach of the duty of obedience and this, coupled with the fact that he was rude and surly, justified summary dismissal. • **Exercise care and skill** (indemnify employer if failure causes him loss). • Perform duties personally. • Act in good faith (honest/faithful service) - i.e. not make secret profit/misappropriate property; not compete with the employer; not disclose confidential information or trade secrets: **Hivac v Park Royal Scientific**. • Act in reasonable manner. • Mutual co-operation, trust and confidence.	• **Pay agreed wages** (whether work available or not). • **Indemnify employee** for liabilities properly incurred. • **Take reasonable care for safety** of employee. Case law establishes that this includes safe plant/machinery; safe system of work; competent/safe staff. • Mutual co-operation, trust and confidence. **No duty to provide work**. Exceptionally, duty if: • payment by commission or piece-work. • rely on publicity or need to maintain skill. **No duty to provide references** (but if do so, must be truthful).

Exam focus

Underpinning question practice

To practice the basics use the following test your understandings:

- Complete/Essential Text – Chapter 4

  Test your understanding 2

  Test your understanding 3.

Wrongful dismissal

<table>
<tr><th>Definition</th><th colspan="2">Minimum notice periods</th></tr>
<tr><td rowspan="4">Employer terminates contract without proper notice or during fixed term (i.e. breach of contract).

Summary dismissal = no notice.</td><td>Continuous employment</td><td>Period of notice</td></tr>
<tr><td>1 month – 2 years</td><td>1 week</td></tr>
<tr><td>2 – 12 years</td><td>1 week per year</td></tr>
<tr><td>12 years +</td><td>12 weeks</td></tr>
<tr><td>Summary dismissal is usually wrongful dismissal unless:
• employee waives rights or accepts payment in lieu of notice.
• employee repudiated contract himself or in fundamental breach (e.g. wilful refusal to obey orders; failure to show professed skill; serious negligence; breach of duty of good faith).</td><td colspan="2">Employees' remedies
Sue in the County Court or High Court for damages:
• usually receive wages for period of notice
• may be additional damages
• duty to mitigate loss
• specific performance generally not granted.</td></tr>
</table>

Exam focus

Underpinning question practice

To practice the basics use the following test your understanding:

- Complete/Essential Text – Chapter 4 Test your understanding 4.

Unfair dismissal

Definition

- Must be continuously employed for one year. Serve grievance notice on employer.
- **Claim** to Employment Tribunal within **three months** of dismissal.
- Employee must **prove** he was **dismissed**. (If does so, presumed unfair).
- **Employer** must **prove reason** for dismissal is permitted.
- The tribunal must be satisfied that the employer acted reasonably.
- If unfair, entitled to reinstatement, re-engagement or compensation

Types of dismissal: s.136 ERA 1996

Contract terminated by employer with or without notice.

Fixed-term contract expired and not renewed.

Constructive dismissal.

Statutory fair reasons for dismissal	Inadmissible reasons for dismissal
• Capabilities/qualifications of employee.	• Victimisation of health and safety complainants.
• Conduct of employee.	• Pregnancy or childbirth.
• Redundancy. Retirement.	• Trade union membership/non-membership/activities.
• Continued employment would contravene statute.	• Assertion of a statutory right.
• Some other substantial reason.	↓
↓	Dismissal for one of these reasons is **automatically unfair**.
Dismissal for one of these reasons is **fair unless employer acted unreasonably** in dismissing for the reason given.	No need to meet length of employment condition.
Must follow proper dismissal procedure.	Additional award of compensation.

Exam focus

Exam standard questions on this area can be found in the revision kit as follows:

- June 2003 – Grounds for dismissal.

Constructive dismissal

Definition	The **employee terminates the contract** with, or without, notice in circumstances which are such that he or she is entitled to terminate it without notice **by reason of the employer's conduct**.
Western Excavating Ltd v Sharp	The employer must be guilty of conduct which is a **significant breach going to the root of the contract** of employment.
Cox Toner (International) Ltd v Crook	If the employee does not resign in the event of the breach, he is deemed to have accepted the breach and waived any rights. However, he need not resign immediately, but may wait until he has found another job.
O'Brien v Associated Fire Alarms	The movement of an employer to a **new location** will normally give rise to a redundancy claim for an employee who does not wish to move, unless his contract contains an **express mobility clause**. Held the employee could resign and claim constructive dismissal.
Simmonds v Dowty Seals Ltd	S had been employed to work on the night shift. When his employer attempted to force him to work on the day shift he resigned. Held: constructively dismissed because the employer had attempt to unilaterally change an express term of the employment contract.

Exam focus

Exam standard questions on this area can be found in the revision kit as follows:

- December 2007 – Dismissal.

Redundancy

Definition - Under s139(1) Employment Rights Act 1996, an employee is redundant if his dismissal is wholly or mainly attributable to the fact that:

- his employer has ceased, or intends to cease, business; or
- the employer's need for employees to do work of that particular kind has ceased or diminished.

The work may have ceased altogether or only in the place where the employee was employed.

Procedure:

Exam focus

Exam standard questions on this area can be found in the revision kit as follows:

- June 2004 – Redundancy.

Remedies

Reinstatement	Re-engagement	Compensation
Employee treated as if not dismissed. Returned to same job with no loss of seniority. Only awarded if applicant wishes and if is practicable.	Comparable employment. Employer's failure to comply with reinstatement or re-engagement results in compensation.	Basic award – as for redundancy. Compensatory – max £66,200. Reduced if complainant contributed to his dismissal.

Not entitled to redundancy payment if unreasonably refused offer of fresh employment (made before old contract expires) to start within four weeks on same or suitable terms.

Calculation of	Redundancy pay/basic award
18-21 years of age	½ week's pay for each year of service
22-40 years of age	1 week's pay for each year of service
41 years plus	1½ week's pay for each year of service
	Maximum is for 20 years' service at £350 per week.

Exam focus

Exam standard questions on this area can be found in the revision kit as follows:

- June 2005 – Remedies.

chapter

5

Agency law

In this chapter

- How the agency relationship arises.
- Authority.
- Liability of the parties.

Exam focus

Agency law is a relatively minor part of the syllabus. It can be examined as an essay question or as part of a question on partnerships or directors.

Exam focus

Exam standard questions on this area can be found in the revision kit as follows:

- December 2001 – Agents' authority
- December 2003 – Agency relationship.

How the agency relationship arises

Definition

An agent (A) is a person who is authorised to act for another, the principal (P), in the making of legal relations with third parties. The relationship can arise in a number of ways:

Express agreement	The agreement can be made orally or in writing.
Implied agreement	The agreement can be implied from the parties' conduct.
Necessity	This requires four conditions to be satisfied: • P's property is entrusted to A • an emergency arises making it necessary for A to act • it is not possible to communicate with P • A acts in the interest of P.
Ratification	This requires P to: • have the contractual capacity to make the contract • have been in existence when the contract was made • be identified when the contract is made • be aware of all the material facts • ratify the whole contract within a reasonable time. **NB A void or illegal contract cannot be ratified.**
Estoppel	This arises where P implies that A is his agent. He is then prevented from denying A's authority – **Freeman & Lockyer v Buckhurst Park Properties**.

Exam focus

Underpinning question practice

To practice the basics use the following test your understanding:

- Complete/Essential Text – Chapter 5

  Test your understanding 1.

Authority

Express	This is authority that P has explicitly given to A.
Implied	An agent has implied authority to do things which: • are reasonably incidental to the performance of an expressly authorised act • an agent occupying that position would usually have authority to do • have not been expressly prohibited by P.
Apparent	Such authority arises where A is held out by P as having authority. The representation by P may arise from: • the appointment of A to an office or position (in which case A has authority to do those things which are usually done by a person occupying that position) • previous dealings (allowing A to make contracts in the past is a representation that A has authority to continue to do so in the future). However, a third party cannot rely on apparent authority when he knows of the lack of actual authority.

Exam focus

Underpinning question practice

To practice the basics use the following test your understanding:

- Complete/Essential Text – Chapter 5 Test your understanding 2.

Liability of the parties

A's fiduciary duty to P:	Disclosed principal - contract is between P and third party. A is not liable or entitled under the contract, unless:
• A must not allow his personal interest to conflict with that of P • A must always act in P's best interests • A must not make a secret profit • A has a duty to account to P for all money and property received. **Remedies for breach of fiduciary duty:** • P can repudiate the contract with the third party • A can be dismissed without notice • P can refuse to pay any money owed to A or recover any money already paid • P can recover any secret profit made or any bribe.	• P is fictitious • A signs contract in own name • A refuses to name P • trade custom dictates personal liability. **Undisclosed principal** – when a third party discovers the existence of P he can elect to treat P or A as bound by the transaction. **P's liability to A:** The agent has the right: • To claim remuneration or commission for services performed • To claim an indemnity against P for all expenses reasonably incurred in carrying out his obligations • To exercise a lien over P's property.

chapter

6

Partnerships

In this chapter

- Partnerships.
- Authority.
- Limited Liability Partnerships Act.

Partnerships

This is an area which although does not come up consistently on the exam, is examined fairly regularly.

Exam focus

Exam standard questions on this area can be found in the revision kit as follows:

- December 2002 – Termination of partnership
- December 2003 – Partnership and liability
- June 2008 – Clare, Dan and Eve.

Definition

A partnership is a relationship which subsists between two or more persons carrying on a business in common with a view to profit.

Types of partners	Types of partnership
• **General partner** – actively involved in the day-to-day business. • **Sleeping partner** – takes no active part in the running of the business. • **Limited partner in a limited partnership** – contributes specific amount of capital. Liability limited to that amount. Can't take part in the management of the firm.	• **Partnership** – governed by Partnership Act 1890. • **Limited partnership** – governed by Limited Partnership Act 1907. There must be at least one partner with unlimited liability. • **Limited liability partnership** – governed by Limited Liability Partnerships Act 2000. Legally separate from its members.

Authority

The partnership agreement is a contract. Partners are subject to the rules of agency when dealing with each other and on behalf of the business.

Actual authority is the authority P has agreed that A should have. It can be:

- express authority which is set out in the agreement between P and A; or
- implied authority. This is where the terms of A's authority are ambiguous or A is given a discretion to act. The law implies authority to enable A to carry out his express duties.

Apparent authority is the authority of A as it appears to others. Can arise from:

- previous dealings;
- by virtue of office or position.

Partners are presumed to have authority to buy and sell goods, engage employees, receive payments of debts due to the firm, and engage a solicitor. Trading partnerships are also presumed to be able borrow money.

Watteau v Fenwick – innkeeper continued to have authority to purchase cigars even though new owners had ordered him not to.

Exam focus

Underpinning question practice

To practice the basics use the following test your understanding:

- Complete/Essential Text – Chapter 6

Test your understanding 1.

Liability of partners	Dissolution of partnership
Every partner is **jointly and severally liable** for any debts and contracts of the business. Outsiders can sue one partner alone or the firm.	• **Without court order** – On expiry of a fixed term or the completion of a specific enterprise.
A **new partner** is not personally liable for anything done before they became a partner.	– One of the partners gives notice. – Death or bankruptcy of a partner.
A **retiring partner** remains liable for debts due at time of retirement. If no notice of retirement is given, firm bound by his actions as still being 'held out' as a partner. Where a third party deals with a partnership after **a change in partners**, all partners of the old firm are still treated as partners until the third party receives notice of the change (e.g. by notice in London Gazette).	• **By Court Order** – Partner has mental disorder or permanent incapacity. – Partner guilty of misconduct. – Partner persistently breaches the partnership agreement. – Business can only be carried on at a loss. – It is just and equitable to do so.

Limited Liability Partnerships Act

Incorporation	• Incorporation document must be delivered to Registrar stating name of LLP, location and address of registered office, names and addresses of members (minimum two). • Must send a Declaration of Compliance that LLP satisfies requirements of the Limited Liability Partnerships Act 2000. • Registrar issues a certificate of incorporation.
Membership	• First members sign incorporation document. Later members join by agreement with existing members. • Membership ceases on death, dissolution or in accordance with agreement with other members. • Rights and duties are set out in membership agreement. If no agreement, governed by Limited Liability Partnership Regulations 2001. • Each member acts as an agent of the LLP.
Designated members	• Perform the administrative and filing duties of the LLP. • Incorporation document specifies who they are. • Must be at least two designated members. If there are none, all members will be designated members.

Name	• Must end with Limited Liability Partnership, llp or LLP. • Rules on choice are the same as for companies.
Taxation	• Members are treated as if they are partners carrying on business in a partnership, i.e. pay income tax not corporation tax.
Liability for debts	• The liability of a member of an LLP to contribute to its debts is limited to his capital contribution. However, there is no requirement for a capital contribution, and any contribution made can be withdrawn at any time. • The fraudulent and wrongful trading provisions of the Insolvency Act 1986 apply to members of LLPs in the same way as they apply to directors of companies.
Differences between LLP & partnership	• Liability of LLP members is limited to the amount of capital they have agreed to contribute. • The LLP must file annual accounts and an annual report with Companies House. • LLP is an artificial legal entity with perpetual succession. It can hold property in its own right, enter into contracts in its own name, create floating charges, sue and be sued.

chapter

7

Corporations and legal personality

In this chapter

- Veil of incorporation.
- Lifting the veil.
- Different types of business organisation.
- Company v partnership.
- Types of company.
- Public company v private company.
- Promoters.
- Pre-incorporation contracts.
- Registration.
- Name of company.

- Articles of association.
- Registers.
- Accounting records and annual return

Exam focus

This chapter introduces company law as a topic and is fundamental. Company law is the largest area of the syllabus and is likely to account for around 50% of the total marks on the paper.

Veil of incorporation

Meaning	Company is separate legal entity (i.e. separate from its shareholders).
Consequences	• Company is liable for its own debts. If it fails, liability of the shareholders is limited to any amount still unpaid on their share capital. • Company has perpetual succession, irrespective of fate of shareholders. • Separation of management from ownership.
Salomon v Salomon & Co Ltd	**Facts:** S transferred his business to a limited company. He was majority shareholder and a secured creditor. Company went into liquidation. Other creditors tried to obtain repayment from S personally. **Held:** S as shareholder and director had no personal liability to creditors and he could be repaid in priority as a secured creditor. This enshrined the concepts of separate legal personality and limited liability in the law.
Lee v Lee's Air Farming	**Facts:** Proprietor of a company (also MD and sole employee) was killed in the course of his employment. Liquidator tried to avoid paying compensation to widow on grounds he was not a separate entity from the company. **Held:** The individual and the company were two separate entities, and the company was liable to pay the compensation.
Macaura v Northern Life Assurance	**Facts:** M sold forest to company he formed, but failed to transfer insurance policy into company's name. Forest was destroyed by fire. **Held:** M unable to claim insurance as the company owned the forest, not him, and company unable to claim since it did not have the insurance policy.

Lifting the veil

'Lifting the veil' allows the courts to look at the identity of the shareholders.

Usual result – members or directors become personally liable for the company's debts.

Examples

- If a public company starts to trade without first obtaining a trading certificate, the directors can be made personally liable for any loss or damage suffered by a third party: S767 CA06.
- Under the Company Directors Disqualification Act 1986, if a director who is disqualified participates in the management of a company, that director will be jointly or severally liable for the company's debts.
- Under Insolvency Act 1986 ('IA86'), members and/or directors found to have carried out **wrongful or fraudulent trading** may be personally liable for losses arising as a result.
- A parent company must prepare **group accounts**, consolidating balance sheets and profit and loss accounts of it and its subsidiaries,allowing investors (and others) to judge the financial position of group as a whole.
- Veil only lifted where '**special circumstances** exist indicating that it is a mere facade concealing the true facts' – **Woolfson v Strathclyde Regional Council**.
- **Sham company**: **Gilford v Horne** - H formed company to run it in competition with G. H had a personal contract with G restraining competition. **Held:** company could be restrained from competition, as H had set it up to evade his own legal obligations.

Exam focus

Exam standard questions on this area can be found in the revision kit as follows:

- June 2008 – Doctrine of separate personality.

Underpinning question practice

To practice the basics use the following test your understanding:

- Complete/Essential Text – Chapter 7

  Test your understanding 1.

Different types of business organisation

Sole trader	• The owner 'is' the business – owns the assets and is liable for all the debts. • No legal formalities are required to set up a sole trader business. • This form of business is inappropriate for large businesses or those involving a degree of risk.
Partnership	Defined by Partnership Act 1890 as the relationship which subsists between persons carrying on a business in common with a view of profit (see below).
Limited liability partnership	• An artificial legal entity with perpetual succession. It can hold property in its own right, enter into contracts in its own name, create floating charges, sue and be sued. • The liability of the members of a limited liability partnership (LLP) is limited to the amount of capital they have agreed to contribute. • The LLP must file annual accounts and an annual report with Companies House.
Company	A corporation is an artificial legal person (see below).

Company v partnership

Company	Partnership
Created by registration - with written constitution.	No special formality required to create.
Separate legal person, i.e. can own property, sue or be sued, and contract in own name.	Not a separate legal person – partners own property, are liable on contracts and liable if sued.
Shares transferable.	Limits on transfer of share (may require dissolution of partnership to enable a partner to realise his share).
Can create both fixed and floating charges.	Can only create fixed charges.
Managed by directors, who may or may not also be shareholders.	Managed by partners, who are also the owners of the business.
Company liable for its debts (no personal liability for shareholders).	Partners personally liable for debts of firm.
Must make information about financial affairs and ownership publicly available.	Private business. No disclosure of results.
Companies pay corporation tax.	Partners pay income tax.
Formal dissolution procedure.	May dissolve by agreement.

Exam focus

Underpinning question practice

To practice the basics use the following test your understandings:

- Complete/Essential Text – Chapter 7

  Test your understanding 2

  Test your understanding 4.

Types of company

- PUBLIC
  - LIMITED BY SHARES
- PRIVATE
  - LIMITED
    - BY SHARES
    - BY GUARANTEE (often for non-profit purposes. Liability of members limited to amount agreed to contribute)
  - UNLIMITED (no need to file accounts)

Public company v private company

	Public companies	Private (limited) companies
Definition	Registered as a public company.	Any company that is not a public company.
Members	Can have a single member.	Can have a single member.
Name	Ends with plc or public limited company.	Ends with Ltd or limited.
Capital	Not less than the authorised minimum (currently £50,000) and, in order to trade, must have allotted shares of at least that amount.	No minimum (or maximum) requirements.
Raising capital	May raise capital by advertising its securities (shares and debentures) as available for public subscription.	Prohibited from offering its securities to the public.
Start of trading	Must obtain trading certificate from Registrar before commence trading.	Can begin from date of incorporation.

Directors	Minimum two.	Minimum one.
Secretary	Must be qualified.	Need not have one.
Accounts	Must file accounts within six months of financial year end.	Need not lay accounts before general meeting. Must file within nine months of year end.
Audit	Accounts must be audited.	Audit not required if turnover below £6.5m.
AGM	Must be held each year.	Need not hold an AGM
Resolutions	Cannot pass written resolutions.	Can pass written resolutions.

Exam focus

Underpinning question practice

To practice the basics use the following test your understanding:

- Complete/Essential Text – Chapter 7

  Test your understanding 3.

Promoters

Definition	No statutory definition. Case law: one who has intention and takes necessary steps to form company. (**Twycross v Grant**). Excludes people acting in professional capacity.
Duties	• Use reasonable care and skill. • Disclose any interest in transactions to company and not make 'secret profit'. • Disclose any benefit acquired to independent board/ shareholders.
Remedies for non-disclosure	• Rescind contract - but not always possible e.g. if third party rights accrued. • Damages - prove loss by company. • Recover profit - prove failure to disclose profit from transaction.

Pre-incorporation contracts

Definition

A contract made by a person acting on behalf of an unformed company.

Position at common law - A company, prior to its incorporation, does not have contractual capacity and the promoter is personally liable.

Kelner v Baxter - Promoter liable for unpaid goods, even though they were used by the company.

s51 CA06 - Reinforces case law. Subject to any agreement to the contrary, the person making the contract is personally liable

Phonogram Ltd. v Lane - Promoter who accepted money on behalf of an unformed company was liable to return it when company not formed.

Protection for the promoter:

- postpone finalising contracts until company is formed
- enter agreement of novation or assign the contract
- buy an 'off the shelf' company, so it is ready to contract
- include term in contract giving company the right to sue under Contracts (Rights of Third Parties) Act 1999
- agree no personal liability for the promoter.

Exam focus

Underpinning question practice

To practice the basics use the following test your understandings:

- Complete/Essential Text – Chapter 7

  Test your understanding 5.
-

Registration

The following documents must be submitted to the Registrar in order to form a company:

Memorandum of association – Signed by all subscribers and stating that they wish to form a company and agree to become members of the company.
Application – The application form must include the proposed name of the company, whether the members will have limited liability (by shares or guarantee), whether the company is to be private or public and details of the registered office.
Articles – The model articles apply if no articles are supplied.
Statement of capital and initial shareholdings – This must state the number of shares, their aggregate nominal value and how much has been paid up.
Statement of guarantee (if applicable) – This states the maximum amount each member undertakes to contribute.
Statement of proposed officers – This gives details of the first directors (and company secretary, if applicable) and their consent to act.
Statement of compliance – This provides confirmation that CA06 has been complied with. It may be made in paper or electronic form.
Registration fee – currently £20.

Public companies	Registrar's duties
In order to obtain a trading certificate, public companies must additionally state: • Nominal value of allotted share capital ≥ £50,000. • At least ¼ nominal value and all premium paid. • Amount of preliminary expenses and any benefits given to promoters.	• **Inspect documents** and ensure Companies Act requirements fulfilled. • **Issue certificate of incorporation** which is conclusive evidence that Companies Act requirements fulfilled. Company exists from date on certificate of incorporation. • **Issue trading certificate** to public companies: s761.
If no trading certificate: • **Criminal offence to carry on business**, but contracts still binding on company. • **Directors personally liable** if company defaults within 21 days of due date.	

Exam focus

Underpinning question practice

To practice the basics use the following test your understanding:

- Complete/Essential Text – Chapter 7

  Test your understanding 7.

Name of company

- Must have limited (Ltd) or public limited company (plc) at end if applicable.
- Cannot be same as another in index of names.
- Cannot use certain words which are illegal or offensive.
- Must have Secretary of State's consent to use certain words e.g. 'England', 'Chartered'.

The Secretary of State can force a company to change its name in the following circumstances.

Reason	**Period**
The name is the same as, or too like, an existing registered name.	12 months
The name gives so misleading an indication of the nature of the company's activities as to be likely to cause harm to the public.	No time limit
Misleading information or undertakings were given when applying for a name that required approval.	5 years

Exam focus

Underpinning question practice

To practice the basics use the following test your understanding:

- Complete/Essential Text – Chapter 7

  Test your understanding 9.

Articles of association

The articles form the company's internal constitution. They:

- Set out the manner in which the company is to be governed, and
- Regulate the relationship between the company and its shareholders.

Model articles

For companies incorporated under CA06, model articles will be prescribed by the Secretary of State.

The model articles apply where a company is formed without registering articles or where the articles registered do not exclude or modify the model articles.

A company:

- may adopt the model articles in full or in part;
- is deemed to have adopted the model articles if there is no express or implied provision to exclude them; or
- may draft its own unique Articles.

Entrenchment

It is possible to entrench some of the articles. This means that a specified procedure (e.g. unanimous consent) may be required to change them.

Exam focus

Underpinning question practice

To practice the basics use the following test your understandings:

- Complete/Essential Text – Chapter 7

  Test your understanding 10

  Test your understanding 11.

Alteration of Articles	Contractual effect of articles
• s21 CA06 – by **special resolution** (75% majority). • Must be '**bona fide in interests of company as a whole**': – for members to decide – court will not interfere unless no reasonable man would consider bona fide – if bona fide - immaterial that happens to inflict hardship or has retrospective operation – will be void if actual fraud/oppression. • Not invalid merely because causes breach of contract - but that does not excuse breach. **Southern Foundries Ltd. v Shirlaw** – MD could sue for breach of contract when articles amended to enable him to be removed.	The articles bind the company and its members to the same extent as if there were covenants on the part of the company and of each member to observe those provisions: S33 CA06. Case law shows that the articles are a contract binding: • company to its members – **Hickman v Kent or Romney Marsh Sheepbreeders Association.** • members to the company – **Pender v Lushington.** • members to one another – **Rayfield v Hands.** Note: Articles are not a contract binding the company to non-members – **Eley v Positive Government Security Life Assurance**, and they do not bind the members in any other capacity – **Beattie v E F Beattie**.

Registers

Register of	Contents
Members	Names, addresses, date became/ceased, number of shares, type, amount paid up.
Directors (and company secretary, if applicable)	Name, occupation, nationality, other directorships within the last five years and date of birth. Should now contain service addresses rather than details of the directors' residential addresses. The service address can be simply 'the company's registered office'. The residential addresses will be withheld from the public register. However, they will remain available to the Registrar and certain specified public bodies and credit reference agencies.
Charges	Name of chargee, type of charge, property charged, amount and date created.
Resolutions and meetings	Records must be kept for a minimum period of 10 years.

The **Registers** must normally be **kept at** the company's **registered office** (although the register of members can be kept where it is made up) and must be a**vailable for public inspection**.

Requests for inspection must provide details about the person seeking the information, the purpose of the request and whether the information will be disclosed to others. The company may apply to the court for an order that it need not comply with the request.

Accounting records and annual return

Accounting records	Annual return
Must contain: • details of all money received and spent • record of assets and liabilities • statement of stocks at end of year • statements of all goods sold and purchased, showing goods and the buyers and sellers (except in the retail trade).	• Must be filed with Registrar annually within 28 days of return date (the anniversary of incorporation). • Contents: – address of registered office – type of company – principal business activities – details of officers – details of issued shares and their holders – details of private company elections to dispense with holding AGMs/laying accounts.

Annual financial statements
• Balance sheet and profit and loss account showing true and fair view • Directors' report stating amount of dividend and likely future developments • Laid before general meeting and copy filed with Registrar

chapter

8

Capital and financing

In this chapter

- Types of capital.
- Share capital terminology.
- Class rights.
- Issuing shares.
- Capital maintenance.
- Distributions.
- Debentures.
- Fixed v floating charges.

Exam focus

This is an area that does come up consistently in the exam as an essay question. There tends to be one question from this area on the exam paper.

Types of capital

	Loan capital	Share capital
Definition	A debenture is a document issued by a company containing an acknowledgment of its indebtedness.	A share is the interest of a shareholder in a company measured by a sum of money.
Voting rights	A creditor of the company, therefore no voting rights.	A member (owner) of the company, therefore voting rights depending on class of shares.
Income	Contractual right to interest irrespective of availability of profits.	Dividends depend on availability of profits.
Liquidation	Priority with respect to repayment.	Receive repayment after creditors, but can participate in surplus assets.

↙ ↓

	Preference shares	Ordinary shares (equity)
Voting rights	None, or restricted.	Full.
Dividend rights	Fixed dividend paid in priority to other dividends, usually cumulative.	Paid after preference dividend. Not fixed.
Surplus on winding up	Prior return of capital, but cannot participate in any surplus.	Entitled to share surplus assets after repayment of preference shares.

Exam focus

Exam standard questions on this area can be found in the revision kit as follows:

- June 2008 – Types of shares.

Underpinning question practice

To practice the basics use the following test your understanding:

- Complete/Essential Text – Chapter 8 Test your understanding 2.

Loan capital versus share capital

	Loan capital	**Share capital**
Definition	A debenture is a document issued by a company containing an acknowledgment of its indebtedness.	A share is the interest of a shareholder in a company measured by a sum of money. It is a bundle of rights and obligations.
Voting rights	A debenture is a creditor of the company and therefore has no voting rights.	A shareholder is a member (owner) of the company and therefore has voting rights, depending on the class of shares held.
Income	A debenture has a contractual right to interest, irrespective of the availability of profits.	Dividends depend on the availability of profits.
Liquidation	A debenture has priority with respect to repayment	Shareholders receive repayment after creditors, but can participate in surplus assets

↙ ↘

	Preference shares	Ordinary shares
Voting rights	None, or restricted	Full
Dividend rights	Fixed dividend paid in priority to other dividends, usually cumulative	Paid after preference dividend. Not fixed.
Surplus on winding up	Prior return of capital, but cannot participate in surplus	Entitled to share surplus assets after repayment of preference shares.

Share capital – terminology

Issued share capital	Issued share capital comprises share capital that has actually been issued, released or sold by the company
Paid up share capital	The amount which shareholders have actually paid on the shares issued.
Called up share capital	The amount of unpaid share capital which has been called for from shareholders but not yet paid.
Uncalled share capital	The amount of unpaid share capital that has not yet been called for from shareolders and therefore also remains unpaid.
Bonus issues	Carried out by using some of the company's reserves to issue fully paid shares to existing shareholders in proportion to their shareholdings. Do not raise any new funds.
Rights issues	New shares offered to existing shareholders in proportion to their shareholdings. Raise new funds. Shares usually offered at discount to current market value (but not at discount to nominal value).

Exam focus

Underpinning question practice

To practice the basics use the following test your understanding:

- Complete/Essential Text – Chapter 8

  Test your understanding 1.

Class rights

Definition

The special rights attached to each class such as dividend rights, distribution of capital on a winding up and voting.

The procedure for varying class rights depends on whether any procedure is specified in the articles:

Is procedure to vary specified?	Method of variation
Yes	Procedure set out in articles must be followed
No	Variation needs special resolution or written consent of 75% in nominal value of the class: s630 CA06.

White v Bristol Aeroplane - Bonus issue is not a variation of class rights.

Greenhalgh v Arderne Cinemas - Subdivision of shares is not a variation of class rights.

Minority protection (s633 CA06)

- Holders of 15% of nominal value of class,
- who did not consent to the variation,
- may ask court to cancel within 21 days of the passing of the resolution.

Issuing shares

Authority	Issue at a premium
• The directors need authority in order to allot shares. • This may be given by the articles, or by passing an ordinary resolution. • The authority must state the maximum number of shares to be allotted and the expiry date for the authority (maximum five years).	S610 CA06 requires any premium to be credited to a share premium account, which may only be used for: • writing off the expenses of the issue of those shares • writing off any commission paid on the issue of those shares • issuing bonus shares.
Issue at a discount	**Paying for shares - public companies**
• Can't issue shares at discount on nominal value: s580 CA06. • **Breach** – issue still valid but allottee must pay up the discount plus interest. • Can issue debentures at a discount if don't have immediate right to convert to shares.	• Subscribers must pay cash for their subscription shares. • Payment for shares must not be in the form of work or services. • Shares cannot be allotted until at least one-quarter of their nominal value and the whole of any premium have been paid. • Non-cash consideration must be received within five years. • Non-cash consideration must be independently valued.

Exam focus

Underpinning question practice

To practice the basics use the following test your understanding:

- Complete/Essential Text – Chapter 8 Test your understanding 3.

Capital maintenance

The capital of a limited company is regarded as a 'buffer fund' for creditors.

The rules on maintenance of capital exist to prevent a company reducing its capital by returning it to its members, whether directly or indirectly. This means that, as a general rule, a limited company cannot reduce its share capital or purchase its own shares. There are, however, some exceptions to this general rule and these are covered later.

Loan capital is not subject to maintenance.

Reduction of capital

Under s641 CA06, a company can reduce its capital at any time, for any reason.

- Reduce/cancel liabilities on partly paid shares; i.e. company gives up claim for money owing.
- Return capital in excess of company's needs; i.e. company reduces assets by repaying cash to shareholders.
- Cancel paid-up capital no longer represented by assets; i.e. company has debit balance on reserves. It writes this off by reducing capital and thereby does not need to make good past losses.

Procedure for public companies:

- Pass a special resolution
- Apply to the court to confirm the special resolution.
- If reduction involves one of the first two methods above, court must require company to settle a list of creditors entitled to object.
- The court must not confirm the reduction until it is satisfied that all creditors have either consented to the reduction or had their debts discharged or secured.
- The company must file documents with the Registrar. If the share capital of a public company falls below £50,000, it must re-register as a private company.

Simplified procedure for private companies:

- Pass a special resolution supported by a solvency statement
- The solvency statement is a statement by each of the directors that the company will be able to meet its debts within the following year.
- A solvency statement made without reasonable grounds is an offence punishable by fine and/or imprisonment.
- Copies of the resolution, solvency statement and a statement of capital must be filed with the Registrar within 15 days.

Exam focus

Exam standard questions on this area can be found in the revision kit as follows:

- December 2002 – Judder Ltd.

Underpinning question practice

To practice the basics use the following test your understanding:

- Complete/Essential Text – Chapter 8

  Test your understanding 4.

Distributions

Company can only make distribution (e.g. pay dividend) out of distributable profits.	The company declares a dividend by passing an ordinary resolution. The amount paid cannot exceed the amount recommended by directors.
Distributable profits = accumulated realised profits less accumulated realised losses (s830 CA06). • Profit/loss - trading or capital. • Accumulated - overall profit/loss, not just one year in isolation. • Realised: – not revaluation – provisions (e.g. depreciation, bad debts) deemed realised.	**Undistributable reserves** • Share premium account • Capital redemption reserve (Used only for bonus issues) • Unrealised profits (i.e. revaluation reserve) • Reserves the company is forbidden to distribute.
Plcs can only declare dividend if net assets will not fall below total of called up share capital and undistributable reserves. Use latest audited accounts to calculate.	**Consequences of unlawful dividend** • Directors liable to make good loss • Shareholders who knew/had reasonable grounds to know must repay. • Auditors liable if paid in reliance on eroneous accounts

Debentures

Definition

A debenture is a document issued by a company containing an acknowledgment of its indebtedness whether charged on the company's assets or not.

All trading companies have implied power to borrow for purpose of business.

Advantages of debentures	Disadvantages of debentures
• Board does not (generally) need authority of general meeting to issue debentures. • As debentures carry no votes they do not dilute/affect control of company. • Interest chargeable against profit before tax. • May be cheaper to service than shares. • No restrictions on issuing at a discount or on redemption.	• Interest must be paid out of pre-tax profits, irrespective of profits of company. • Default may precipitate liquidation and/or administration if secured. • High gearing will affect share price.

Exam focus

Underpinning question practice

To practice the basics use the following test your understanding:

- Complete/Essential Text – Chapter 8

  Test your understanding 6.

Fixed v floating charges

Fixed charge	Floating charge
A fixed charge is a legal or equitable mortgage on a specific asset (e.g. land), which prevents the company dealing with the asset without the consent of the mortgagee.	A floating charge is an equitable charge on a class of assets present and future that will change from time to time and which company can use without the chargee's consent (e.g. stock): **Re Yorkshire Woolcombers Association.**
A fixed charge has three main characteristics: • it is on an identified asset • the asset is intended to be retained permanently in the business • the company has no general freedom to deal with (e.g. sell) the asset.	A floating charge has three main characteristics: • it is on a class of assets, present and future • the assets within the class will change from time to time • the company has freedom to deal with the charged assets in the ordinary course of its business.

Exam focus

Exam standard questions on this area can be found in the revision kit as follows:

- June 2001 – Debentures, fixed and floating charges.

Advantages and disadvantages	Crystallisation
Advantages of floating charge to company Company can deal freely with the assets. Wider class of assets can be charged. **Disadvantages of floating charge to chargee** Value of security uncertain until crystallises. Lower priority than fixed charge. Liquidator can ignore if created within 12 months of winding up.	A floating charge does not attach to any particular asset until crystallisation. **Crystallisation** means the company can no longer deal freely with the assets. It occurs in following cases: • liquidation • company ceases to carry on business • any event specified (e.g. company unable to pay debts; company fails to look after property; company fails to maintain stock levels).
Priority	**Registration**
• Equal charges - first created has priority. • Fixed charge - priority over floating charge. • An unregistered registerable charge has no priority over a registered charge. Can prohibit creation of later charge with priority, but only effective if subsequent chargee has notice of prohibition as well as charge.	Notify **Registrar** within **21 days** of creation. **Failure:** • renders charge void against liquidator • fine on company and every officer in default • money secured becomes immediately repayable. **Who can register?** The company or the chargeholder.

Exam focus

Underpinning question practice

To practice the basics use the following test your understanding:

- Complete/Essential Text – Chapter 8

  Test your understanding 7.

chapter

9

Directors

In this chapter

- Types of director.
- Appointment.
- Disqualification.
- Removal.
- Duties.

Exam focus

There is likely to be one question (or possibly two) on directors in the exam paper.

Types of director

Director	'Any person occupying the position of director by whatever name called': s250 CA06. The decision as to whether someone is a director is therefore based on their function, not their title.
Managing director	The model articles allow the board to delegate to the MD any powers they see fit. MD has dual role – member of board and also executive officer. **Freeman & Lockyer v Buckhurst Park Properties** – the MD has the apparent authority to enter into all contracts of a commercial nature.
Shadow director	'A person in accordance with whose directions or instructions the directors of the company are accustomed to act': s251 CA06. Not a shadow director if advice is given only in a professional capacity.
Executive director	Likely to be a full-time employee involved in management. Contract must be available for inspection by members.
Non-executive director	Part-time. Brings outside expertise to board. Not an employee. Exerts control over executive directors.
Chairman of board	Chairs meetings of board. Acts as spokesman for the company.

Exam focus

Exam standard questions on this area can be found in the revision kit as follows:

- June 2008 – Types of directors.

Appointment

First directors	• Minimum: public = two; private = one. • Maximum – no statutory maximum, but articles may specify.
Appointment procedure	• Usually appointed by the existing directors or by ordinary resolution. • A director's actions are valid notwithstanding that his appointment was defective: s161 CA06.
Model articles for public companies	• First AGM all retire and offer themselves for re-**election by ordinary resolution**. • Each AGM one half retire (most senior). Can be re-elected. • Casual vacancies are filled by board until next AGM when must stand for election.
Publicity	Notify Companies House within 14 days of new appointments and any changes in particulars. Also enter details in Register of Directors.
Service contracts	• Cannot exceed two years unless they have been approved by the shareholders by ordinary resolution: s188 CA06. • Must be kept open for inspection at the registered office.
Compensation for loss of office	• Gratuitous payments must be disclosed to all members and approved by ordinary resolution.

Disqualification

Articles	May require directors to hold shares. If so, must obtain within 2 months of becoming director.
Model articles	Vacate office if become bankrupt or insane.
Company Directors (Disqualification) Act 1986	
Effect of court order	Cannot be concerned in management of company directly/indirectly or act as liquidator, receiver or promoter. Maximum 15 years, unless otherwise stated.
Grounds for disqualification	• Convicted of serious offence in connection with management of company. • Persistent breach of CA06 – e.g. failure to file returns – maximum 5 years. • Fraudulent or wrongful trading. • An investigation by the Department for Business, Enterprise and Regulatory Reform (formerly the DTI) has held unfit to be concerned in management of company.
Breach of disqualification order	• Criminal offence (fine and imprisonment). • Personally liable for debts of company while so acting.

Exam focus

Exam standard questions on this area can be found in the revision kit as follows:

- June 2005 – Disqualification.

Removal

Special notice (28 days) of resolution by persons wishing to remove director.
The company must forward a copy of the resolution to the director concerned.

Notice of meeting to director and all members entitled to attend and vote

Director can require company to circulate written representations to members

At the meeting, director can read out representations if no time for prior circulation
Director must be allowed to attend and speak
Ordinary resolution: s168 CA06

Exam focus

Exam standard questions on this area can be found in the revision kit as follows:

- December 2003 – Appointing and removing directors.

Underpinning question practice

To practice the basics use the following test your understanding:

- Complete/essential – Chapter 9

  Test your understanding 1.

Duties

The previous common law rules have now been replaced by the specific statutory duties provided in the Companies Act 2006. However, the old case law still has relevance in interpreting the new legislation and illustrating its application: s.170.

Duty to act within powers: 171 – A director should only use his powers for the purpose for which they were given.
Duty to promote the success of the company: s172 – A director must act in good faith for the benefit of the members as a whole.

Duty to exercise independent judgment: **s173**

Duty to exercise reasonable care, skill and diligence: s174 – The standard expected of a director is that of a reasonably diligent person with:

- the general knowledge, skill and experience that could reasonably be expected of a director, and
- the actual knowledge, skills and experience held by the director.

Re City Equitable Fire Insurance (1925) established that:

- Directors are not bound to give continuous attention to the affairs of their company. However, they should attend board meetings whenever able to do so.
- In the absence of suspicious circumstances, directors may rely on employees to perform the functions that may properly be delegated.

Duty to avoid conflicts of interest: s175

Duty not to accept benefits from third parties: s176

Duty to declare interest in proposed transaction or arrangement: s177 – This declaration can be made in writing, at a board meeting or by a general notice that he has an interest in a third party. **IDC v Cooley (1972)** illustrates that an individual may still be subject to this duty even after he ceases to be a director.

Breach of directors' duties

Duties are owed to the company as a whole, not to individual members: **Percival v Wright (1902).**

Breach of duty may carry the following consequences:

- The director may be required to make good any loss suffered by the company.
- Contracts entered into between the company and the director may be rendered voidable.
- Any property taken by the director from the company can be recovered from him if still in his possession.

- Property may be recovered directly from a third party, unless that third party acquired it for value and in good faith.
- An injunction may be an appropriate remedy where the breach has not yet occurred.

S239 CA06 states that the company can ratify a breach of duty by passing an ordinary resolution.

Exam focus

Exam standard questions on this area can be found in the revision kit as follows:

- June 2004 – Kells Ltd.

Underpinning question practice

To practice the basics use the following test your understanding:

- Complete/essential – Chapter 9

  Test your understanding 2.

chapter

10

Corporate administration

In this chapter

- Company secretary.
- Auditor.
- Duties, resignation and removal.
- Types of meeting.
- Who can call a meeting?
- Notice.
- Resolutions.
- Procedure at meetings.

Exam focus

Questions on this area of the syllabus are likely to appear occasionally in the exam.

Company secretary

- Every public company must have a secretary. Private companies are not obliged to have a secretary.
- Secretary of public company must be qualified:
  - held office of company secretary in plc for at least 3 out of preceding 5 years or
  - is a solicitor, barrister or member of ICAEW, ACCA, CIMA, ICSA, CIPFA or
  - by virtue of other position/qualification appears capable.
- The secretary is usually appointed and removed by the directors.

Duties	Authority to bind company in contract
• Documentation in order, returns made to Registrar and registers kept. • Notice and minutes of meetings. • Countersigning documents to which company seal affixed.	• Actual. • Apparent re contracts of administrative nature: **Panorama Development v Fidelis Furnishing Fabrics** Company secretary ordered services for his own, not company's, use. Held that the contract was binding on the company as the contract was of the sort a company secretary should be able to carry out.

Exam focus

Underpinning question practice

To practice the basics use the following test your understanding:

- Complete/Essential Text – Chapter 10
  Test your understanding 1.

Auditor

Appointment	
• Generally appointed by the shareholders by ordinary resolution, but directors can appoint first auditor and fill casual vacancies. • Qualifications - member of Recognised Supervisory Body and eligible under rules. • Must not be - officer/employee of company or partner of officer/employee.	• A company must inform the Secretary of State if it has failed to appoint. The Secretary of State then has powers to appoint.

Duties, resignation and removal

Removal	Duties
By **ordinary resolution with special notice** at a general meeting. (Cannot remove by written resolution). **Resignation** • May resign by **written notice** to company. • Auditor **may require directors to call meeting within 28 days** if there are circumstances connected with resignation.	**Statutory duty** to audit and report to members on whether: • proper books of accounting records have been kept, and proper returns adequate for their audit have been received from branches not visited by them • the accounts are in agreement with the books of account and returns. **Powers** • Receive notice of, attend and speak at general meetings. • Access to books, accounts, vouchers. • Require information/explanations from officers and employees. (Criminal offence to fail to provide information requested, unless not reasonably practicable to do so).

Exam focus

Underpinning question practice

To practice the basics use the following test your understanding:

- Complete/Essential Text – Chapter 10 Test your understanding 2.

Types of meeting

Annual general meeting

Timing	Public companies must hold an AGM within the six months following their financial year end: s336. Private companies are not required to hold an AGM.
Failure to hold	The company and every officer in default can be fined if an AGM is not held. Any member can apply to the Department for Business, Enterprise and Regulatory Reform to convene the meeting.
Notice	**21 days' notice** is required unless every member entitled to attend and vote agrees to a shorter period. Must state that the meeting is an AGM.
Business	Usual business includes consider accounts, appoint auditors, elect directors and declare dividends.
Resolutions	Members holding at least 5% of the voting rights (or at least 100 members holding on average £100 paid-up capital) have the right to propose a resolution and require the company to circulate details to all members. If the request is received before the financial year end, the members are not required to cover the costs of circulation. Otherwise, the members requesting the statement must deposit a sum to cover the company's costs.

General meeting

Timing	Held whenever required. Must be held by a plc if a serious loss of capital has occurred, i.e. net assets have fallen to less than half of the paid up share capital.
Notice	At least **14 days.**
Business	The person who requisitions the meeting sets the agenda.

Class meeting

Purpose	Meeting of a class of shareholders, usually to consider a variation of their class rights.
Procedure	Notice, etc as for general meetings.
Quorum	Two persons holding or representing by proxy at least 1/3 in nominal value of the issued shares of the class in question.

Who can call a meeting?

Directors	Articles usually delegate power to directors.
Members	• May require directors to call GM if hold 10% paid up voting capital, or in the case of a private company, 5% of the paid up voting capital if more than 12 months has elapsed since the last GM: s303. • Directors must call within 21 days of receiving requisition. • Meeting must take place within 28 days of the notice convening the meeting. • If the directors do not call a meeting, the members who requested the meeting (or any members holding over 50% of the total voting rights) may themselves call a meeting to take place within three months of the initial request and recover their expenses from the company.
Resigning auditor	May require directors to convene so he can explain the reasons for his resignation:
Court	On application of director/member where otherwise impracticable. E.g. to break a deadlock.

Notice

Who must receive notice?	Every member and every director: s310.
Failure to give notice	Accidental failure to give notice to one or more persons does not invalidate the meeting: s313.
Contents of notice	Date, time and place of the meeting. The general nature of the business to be transacted. The text of any special resolutions.
Length of notice period	**AGM – 21 days** Less if every member entitled to attend and vote agrees. **GM – 14 days** Less if members holding at least 95% of shares agree. (Where company is private, can be reduced to 90%).
Special notice	Requires 28 days' notice. Required for the removal of a director or auditor

Exam focus

Exam standard questions on this area can be found in the revision kit as follows:

- Pilot paper – Types of meetings
- December 2001 – Calling and voting.

Resolutions

Type:	% required to pass:	To Registrar?	Purpose of resolution:
Special	75	Yes – within 15 days	Alter name, objects or articles. Reduce share capital. Wind up company.
Ordinary	Simple Majority	Only if required by statute	Used whenever the law or the articles do not require a special resolution.
Written (private companies only)	Same majority as required in GM	Yes if 75% majority required.	The purpose can be anything apart from resolutions requiring special notice. Members cannot revoke their agreement. The date of the resolution is the date when the necessary majority has been reached. The resolution must be passed within 28 days from its circulation.

Exam focus

Exam standard questions on this area can be found in the revision kit as follows:

- December 2000 – Resolutions.

Underpinning question practice

To practice the basics use the following test your understanding:

- Complete/Essential Text – Chapter 10

  Test your understanding 3.

Procedure at meetings

A **quorum** is the minimum number of members that needs to be present at a meeting in order to validate business. It is generally two persons; members or proxies: s318 CA06.

Voting is by a **show of hands** initially, unless a poll is demanded. A show of hands means one member one vote, irrespective of the number of shares held.

A **poll** may be demanded by members holding at least 10% of the total voting rights (or by not fewer than 5 members having the right to vote on the resolution). A poll means one vote per share. The result of a poll replaces the result of the previous show of hands.

Quoted companies must publish the results of polls on their website: s341 CA06.

Members have a statutory right under s 324 CA06 to appoint one or more persons as their '**proxy**'. A proxy can attend meetings, vote and speak on behalf of the member for whom he is acting.

chapter

11

Insolvency

In this chapter

- Voluntary liquidation.
- Members' voluntary liquidation.
- Creditors' voluntary liquidation.
- Compulsory liquidation.
- Application of assets.
- Administration.

Exam focus

A question on insolvency is likely to appear occasionally.

Voluntary liquidation: s.84 IA 86

When a voluntary liquidation may occur:

- Where period fixed for duration of company expires or an event occurs upon which the articles provide that a company should be wound up and an ordinary resolution passed.
- Special resolution passed.

Types of voluntary liquidation:

- Members' voluntary liquidiation– if company is solvent.
- Creditors' voluntary liquidation– if company is insolvent.

A members' voluntary liquidation must be converted in a creditors' voluntary liquidation if the liquidator discovers that the company's debts will not be paid in full.

Members' voluntary liquidation

The directors make a declaration of solvency stating that they are of the opinion that the company will be able to pay its debts within 12 months. It is a criminal offence to make a false declaration.

Winding up commences from the date of passing of the appropriate resolution.

The members **appoint a named insolvency practitioner as liquidator**.

The liquidator is responsible for realising the assets and distributing the proceeds.

The liquidator presents his report to a **final meeting** of the members

The liquidator **informs the Registrar** of the final meeting and submits a copy of his report.

The Registrar registers the report and the company is **dissolved three months later**.

Creditors' voluntary liquidation

Winding up commences from the passing of the appropriate resolution.

There is no declaration of solvency as the company is insolvent.
A meeting of creditors must be held within 14 days of the resolution to liquidate.
The directors must submit a **statement of the company's affairs**.

Both the members and the creditors have the right to **appoint a named insolvency practitioner as liquidator**. In the event of a dispute, the creditors' nominee prevails. The members and creditors may appoint up to five persons to serve on a **liquidation committee**.

The liquidator is responsible for realising the assets and distributing the proceeds.

The liquidator presents his report to the **final meetings** of members and creditors.

The liquidator **informs the Registrar** of the final meeting(s) and submits a copy of his report.

The Registrar registers the report and the company is dissolved **three months later**.

Exam focus

Exam standard questions on this area can be found in the revision kit as follows:

- June 2004 – Winding up.

Underpinning question practice

To practice the basics use the following test your understanding:

- Complete/Essential Text – Chapter11

  Test your understanding 1.

Compulsory liquidation

Grounds for winding-up: s.122 IA86	Petitioners
• Company has passed **special resolution** to be wound up by the court. • Public co **hasn't been issued with trading certificate within a year** of registration. • Company has **not commenced business within a year** of being incorporated. • The company is **unable to pay its debts**: – a creditor who is owed at least £750 has served a written demand for payment within three weeks and the company has failed to pay the sum due – the court is satisfied that the company is unable to pay its debts. • It is **just and equitable** to wind up.	• The company itself. • The Official Receiver. • The Department for Business, Enterprise and Regulatory Reform. • A contributory = any person who is liable to contribute to the assets of the company when it is being wound up (contributory must prove that the company is solvent). • A creditor owed at least £750. **Effect of winding-up** • All actions for the recovery of debt against the company are stopped. • Company ceases to carry on business except where it is necessary for winding up. • Powers of directors cease. • Employees automatically made redundant.

Exam focus

Exam standard questions on this area can be found in the revision kit as follows:

- December 2004 – Grounds for winding up.

Underpinning question practice

To practice the basics use the following test your understanding:

- Complete/Essential Text – Chapter 11 Test your understanding 2.

Application of assets

The liquidator must repay debts in the following order.

- Fixed charge-holders.
- Expenses of liquidation.
- Preferential creditors.
  - wages or salaries due in the four months preceding the commencement of winding up (maximum £800 per employee).
  - all accrued holiday pay.
- Floating charge-holders.
- Unsecured creditors (including HMRC) – rank equally amongst themselves.
- Post-liquidation interest.
- Members - declared but unpaid dividends.
- Members - return of capital.
- Any surplus to be distributed to members.

Exam focus

Underpinning question practice

To practice the basics use the following test your understanding:

- Complete/Essential Text – Chapter 11 Test your understanding 3.

Administration

Purposes	Consequences of administration
• Rescue a company in financial difficulty. • Achieve a better result for the creditors than would be likely if the company were to be wound up. • Realise property to pay one or more secured creditors. **Who can appoint an administrator?** • The **court** in response to a petition by e.g. a creditor. • The **holder of a floating charge**. • The company or its directors provided that winding up has not already begun.	• The rights of creditors to enforce debts remain suspended. • All company documents must state that company is in administration and the name of the administrator. • Any petition for winding up is dismissed. • No resolution may be passed to wind up the company. • A qualified insolvency practitioner is appointed to administer the affairs of the company.

Carrying out the administration	Ending the administration
• Administrator must send a **statement of proposals** to all creditors and members. • The proposal must be presented to a meeting of creditors at which they will decide whether to approve them. • If the meeting does not approve the proposals, the court may dismiss the order or make such provisions as it sees fit. • If the meeting approves the proposals the administrator can carry them out.	• The administrator may apply to the court for discharge at any time. He must make an application when the purpose of the order has been achieved or is incapable of being achieved. • The administration must be **completed within 12 months** of the date on which it commenced. This term can be extended with consent of the court or the creditors.

chapter

12

Corporate governance

In this chapter

- Interaction of corporate governance and company law.
- The Cadbury Committee.
- The Greenbury Report.
- The Hampel Report.
- The 1998 Combined Code.
- The Turnbull Report.
- The Higgs Report (2003).
- The Smith Report (2003).
- Main provisions of the Combined Code on Corporate Governance.
- Legal regulation of corporate governance.

Exam focus

Governance is new to the law syllabus.

Definition

Corporate governance is the system by which companies are directed and controlled.

Interaction of corporate governance and company law

	Compliance requirements	Penalties
Law	The law must always be obeyed.	Penalties for infringement of the law may be civil or criminal. Civil remedies may allow the company to recover funds from directors who breach their legal obligations. A fine and/or imprisonment might result from certain criminal infringements.
Corporate governance	The Stock Exchange rules require listed companies to comply with the Combined Code (see below). If a listed company does not comply, it must specify the provisions with which it has not complied, and give reasons for its non-compliance. Unlisted companies are under no obligation to comply, although it is considered best practice to do so.	There are no formal penalties for non-compliance. However, the company may suffer loss of reputation and receive bad publicity.

Exam focus

Underpinning question practice

To practice the basics use the following test your understanding:

- Complete/Essential Text – Chapter 12 Test your understanding 1.

The Cadbury Committee

Set up by?	The Financial Reporting Council, the London Stock Exchange and the accountancy profession.
Objective	To help raise the standards of corporate governance and the level of confidence in financial reporting and auditing by setting out clearly the respective responsibilities of those involved and what was expected of them.
Publication	**A Code of Best Practice (1992)** was designed to achieve the necessary high standards of corporate behaviour.
Recommended	• It is desirable to separate the role of chief executive and chairman. • The board should include sufficient non-executive directors for their views to carry significant weight. • The appointment of an audit committee to review the financial statements before their submission to the full board. • A remuneration committee consisting wholly or mainly of non-executive directors should set the remuneration of executive directors. • A 3-year maximum term on executive directors' service contracts.
Outcome	The Stock Exchange required all listed companies to state whether they had complied with the Code and to give reasons for any areas of non-compliance.

The Greenbury Report

Set up by?	The CBI in 1995.
Objective	To draw up guidelines on directors' remuneration, which was perceived to be excessive and did not seem to be linked to the company's performance.
Publication	A code of best practice in determining and accounting for directors' remuneration.
Outcome	All listed companies registered in the UK were required to comply with the Code. Their annual reports had to include a statement about their directors' remuneration. Any areas of non-compliance had to be explained and justified.

The Hampel Report

Issued	January 1998.
Objective	To restrict the regulatory burden facing companies and substitute broad principles (rather than detailed regulations) where practicable.
Summary	A board must not approach the various corporate governance requirements in a compliance mentality: the so-called 'tick-box' approach. Good corporate governance is not achieved by satisfying a checklist. Directors must comply with the substance as well as the letter of all best practice pronouncements.
Outcome	After publishing its report, the Hampel Committee drew up a single Combined Code of Best Practice, incorporating the Cadbury, Greenbury and Hampel recommendations.

The 1998 Combined Code

Objective	To combine the accepted principles and best practice guidelines of Cadbury, Greenbury and Hampel into a single code.
Outcome	The Stock Exchange Listing Rules require a listed company in the UK to include the following in its annual report and accounts. • A narrative statement of **how it has applied the principles** set out in the Combined Code, providing explanation which enables its shareholders to evaluate how the principles have been applied. • A statement as to **whether or not it has complied** throughout the accounting period with the Combined Code provisions. If it has not complied, it must specify the provisions with which it has not complied, and give **reasons for any non-compliance**. This approach to compliance is known as 'comply or explain'.
Revised	2003 and 2006
Appendices	Turnbull, Higgs and Smith Reports (see below)

The Turnbull Report

Issued	In 1999 by the ICAEW
Objective	To give additional guidance to listed companies on how to implement the provisions of the Combined Code dealing with internal control.
Summary	The board should look forward and not just consider past performance. Companies should keep their shareholders informed about risks. Directors should be aware that the company must continually adapt to its changing environment. Risks should be reviewed regularly.

The Higgs Report (2003)

Objective	To develop guidelines for making non-executive directors more effective.
Outcome	Most of the report's recommendations were either written into the 2003 Combined Code or included in the best practice guidelines that are appended to it.

The Smith Report (2003)

Objective	To give guidance to company boards in making suitable arrangements for their audit committees and to assist directors serving on audit committees in carrying out their role.

Main provisions of the Combined Code on Corporate Governance

Directors

- Every company should be headed by a board.
- The board should include a balance of executive and non-executive directors, such that no individual or small group of individuals can dominate the board's decision-taking.
- No one individual should have unfettered powers of decision.
- Formal and transparent procedure for the appointment of new directors. All directors should receive induction on joining the board and should regularly update and refresh their skills and knowledge.
- The board should be supplied with timely information in a form and of a quality appropriate to enable it to discharge its duties.
- The board should undertake a formal and rigorous annual evaluation of its own performance and that of its committee and individual directors.
- All directors should be submitted for re-election at regular intervals, subject to continued satisfactory performance. The board should ensure planned and progressive refreshing of the board.
- The following persons cannot be regarded as independent:
  - anyone who has been an employee of the company in the previous five years
  - anyone who has had a material business relationship with the company in the previous three years
  - anyone who has served on the board for more than nine years.

Directors' remuneration

- Levels of remuneration should be sufficient to attract, retain and motivate directors of the quality required to run the company successfully, but a company should avoid paying more than is necessary for this purpose. A significant proportion of executive directors' remuneration should be structured so as to link rewards to corporate and individual performance.
- There should be a formal and transparent procedure for developing policy on executive remuneration and for fixing the remuneration packages of individual directors. No director should be involved in deciding his or her own remuneration.
- Service contracts and notice periods should not exceed one year.

Accountability and audit

- The board should present a balanced and understandable assessment of the company's position and prospects.
- The board should maintain a sound system of internal control to safeguard shareholders' investment and the company's assets.
- The board should establish formal and transparent arrangements for considering how they should apply the financial reporting and internal control principles and for maintaining an appropriate relationship with the company's auditors.
- The board should establish an audit committee of at least three members, who should all be independent NEDs. At least one member should have recent and relevant financial experience.
- Appointments should be for up to three years, extendable twice, provided the individual continues to be independent.
- The committee should meet at least three times during the year.

Exam focus

Underpinning question practice

To practice the basics use the following test your understanding:

- Complete/Essential Text – Chapter 12 Test your understanding 2.

Legal regulation of corporate governance

Model articles	Set out the internal constitution of the company, e.g. allowing the company and/or the board to negotiate directors' service contracts.
CA 2006	Provides the main framework for the legislation affecting companies. Specifies that a director's service contract cannot exceed two years unless first approved by the members. Specifies the duties that directors owe to their companies.
Case law	Provides the interpretation of the relevant legislation and demonstrates how the Act is applied to specific circumstances.
Insolvency Act 1986	Established liability for wrongful trading and fraudulent trading. Permits the liquidator to set aside transactions at an undervalue or where the company has given a preference.
Company Directors Disqualification Act 1986	Allows the court to disqualify someone from being a director if they: • have persistently breached the companies' legislation • are found to be unfit or • are convicted of an indictable offence in connection with the promotion, formation, management or liquidation of a company.
Criminal Justice Act 1993	Contains the legislation on insider dealing.

Exam focus

Exam standard questions on this area can be found in the revision kit as follows:

- Pilot paper – Meaning of corporate governance and relationships between executive and non-executive directors.

Underpinning question practice

To practice the basics use the following test your understanding:

- Complete/Essential Text – Chapter 12

  Test your understanding 3.

chapter

13

Fraudulent behaviour

In this chapter

- Insider dealing.
- Money laundering.
- Fraudulent and wrongful trading.

Exam focus

Insider dealing has previously been examined on a number of occasions as a scenario question.

Insider dealing

Legislation	Contained in **Part V Criminal Justice Act 1993**.
The offences	An individual who has information as an insider is guilty of insider dealing if: • they **deal in securities** that are price-affected in relation to the information • they **encourage another person to deal** (knowing or having reasonable cause to believe that dealing would take place) • they **disclose the information** (otherwise than in the proper performance of the functions of their employment, office or profession).
Insider	A person has information as an insider if it is, and he knows that it is, inside information or he has it, and knows that he has it, from an inside source.
Inside information	Inside information is information which: • **relates to particular securities** or to a particular issuer of securities • **is specific** or precise • has **not** been made **public** • if made public would be likely to have a **significant effect on the price**.

Inside source	A person has information from an inside source if and only if: • he has it through being a director, employee, or shareholder of an issuer of securities ('primary insider') • he has it through having access to the information by virtue of his employment, office or profession ('primary insider') • he has the information from a person who is within either of these categories ('secondary insider').
Defences	• Didn't expect the dealing to result in a profit (or the avoidance of a loss) attributable to the fact that the information in question was price-sensitive. • Believed on reasonable grounds that the information had been widely disclosed. • Would have done what he did even if he had not had the information.
Consequences	Imprisonment (6 months' summary or 7 years' indictment) and a fine. Transactions remain valid and enforceable. No civil compensation. Director breaches fiduciary duty and is liable to account for any profit made.

Exam focus

Exam standard questions on this area can be found in the revision kit as follows:

- Pilot paper – Insider Dealing
- June 2008 – Sid and Vic.

Underpinning question practice

To practice the basics use the following test your understanding:

- Complete/Essential Text – Chapter 13 Test your understanding 1.

Money laundering

Definition	Money laundering is the process by which the proceeds of crime are converted into assets which appear to have a legal rather than an illegal source.
Legislation	**Proceeds of Crime Act 2002**
Phases	• **Placement** – the initial disposal of the proceeds of criminal activity into an apparently legitimate business activity or property. • **Layering** – the transfer of money from business to business, or place to place, in order to conceal its initial source. • **Integration** – the culmination of the previous procedures through which the money takes on the appearance of coming from a legitimate source.
Offences	• Laundering – concealing, disguising, or transferring criminal property. • Failure to report – individuals (such as accountants and solicitors) may be guilty of an offence of failing to disclose knowledge or suspicion of money laundering where they know or suspect, or have reasonable grounds for knowing or suspecting, that another person is engaged in laundering the proceeds of crime. • Tipping off – making a disclosure likely to prejudice an investigation.
Penalties	Money laundering – maximum 14 years' imprisonment. Failure to report and tipping off – maximum of five years' imprisonment and/or a fine.

Exam focus

Exam standard questions on this area can be found in the revision kit as follows:

- December 2005 – Money laundering.

Underpinning question practice

To practice the basics use the following test your understanding:

- Complete/Essential Text – Chapter 13 Test your understanding 2.

Fraudulent and wrongful trading

	Fraudulent trading	Wrongful trading
Definition	Fraudulent trading occurs where the company's business is **carried on with intent to defraud** creditors or for any fraudulent purpose: s213 IA 1986. Note high burden of proof involved in proving dishonesty.	On winding-up it appears to court that company has gone into insolvent liquidation and, before start of winding up, director knew or ought to have concluded there was no **reasonable prospect that company could avoid insolvent liquidation**: S.214 IA 1986.
Who is liable?	Any persons knowingly party to the carrying on of the business.	Directors and shadow directors.
Consequences	• Contribute to company's assets. • 15 years' disqualification under CDDA86. • Fine and/or imprisonment.	• Contribute to company's assets. • 15 years' disqualification under CDDA86.
Case law	**R v Grantham** – ordering goods on credit knowing that they would not be paid for. Held: fraudulent trading.	**Re Produce Marketing Consortium** – defence that took all reasonable steps to minimise loss to creditors.

Exam focus

Exam standard questions on this area can be found in the revision kit as follows:

- June 2001 – Wrongful trading.

Underpinning question practice

To practice the basics use the following test your understanding:

- Complete/Essential Text – Chapter 13

  Test your understanding 3.

Index

A

B

C

D

J

K

L

M

N

O

P

R

S